'That's Really Sweet'

by
David Orme

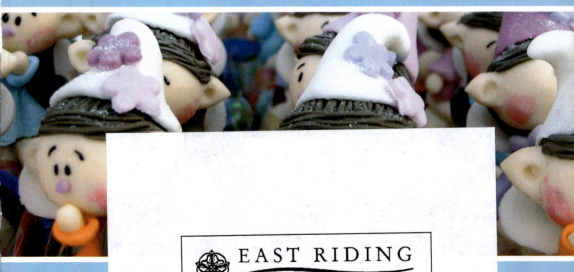

Thunderbolts

'That's Really Sweet'
by David Orme

Illustrated by Maria Taylor

Published by Ransom Publishing Ltd.
Radley House, 8 St. Cross Road, Winchester, Hants. SO23 9HX, UK
www.ransom.co.uk

ISBN   978 178127 067 7

First published in 2013

Contents

4

'That's Really Sweet': The Facts

Sweet shop, 1927 ...

... a chocolate shop today.

Drinking chocolate, 1775

World War 2: chocolate rationing

Waiting for sugar

What's in a bar of chocolate?

Milk

Sugar

Cocoa powder

Fat

13

All made of chocolate!

15

How to make tasty truffles

What you need:

cream

Melt the chocolate ...

Add the cream and let it set ...

Make your truffles!

How to make honey

What you need:

The bee drinks nectar from flowers.

The bee spits out the nectar.
This turns it into honey.

The bees store the honey.

Collect the honey.

Are sweets good for you?

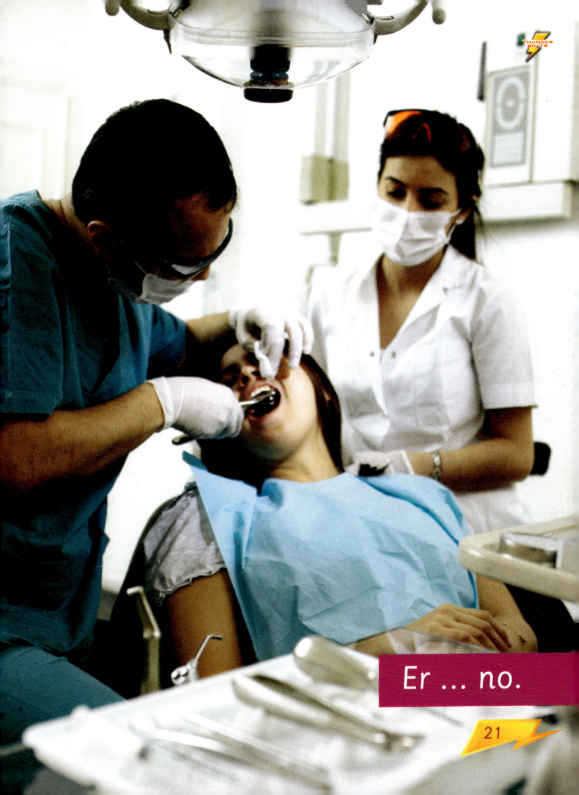

Er ... no.

Fair trade?

FAIRTRADE

Fair ...

Not fair ...

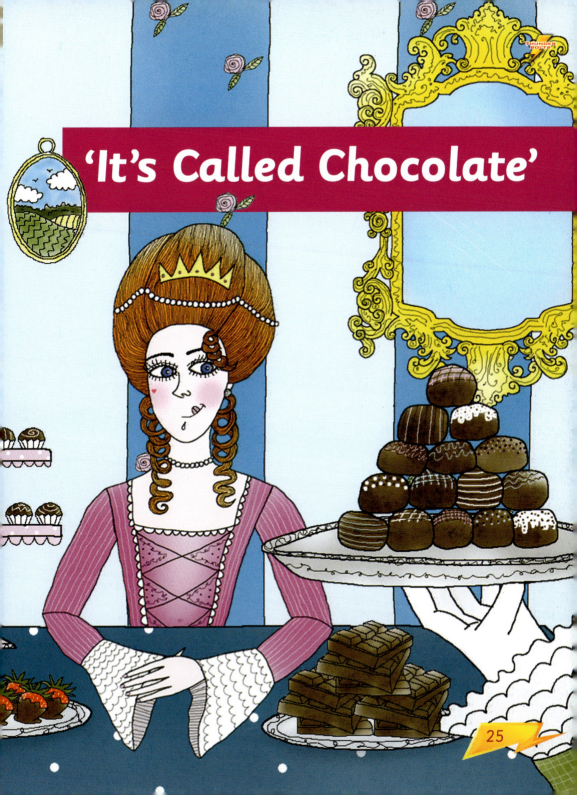

'It's Called Chocolate'

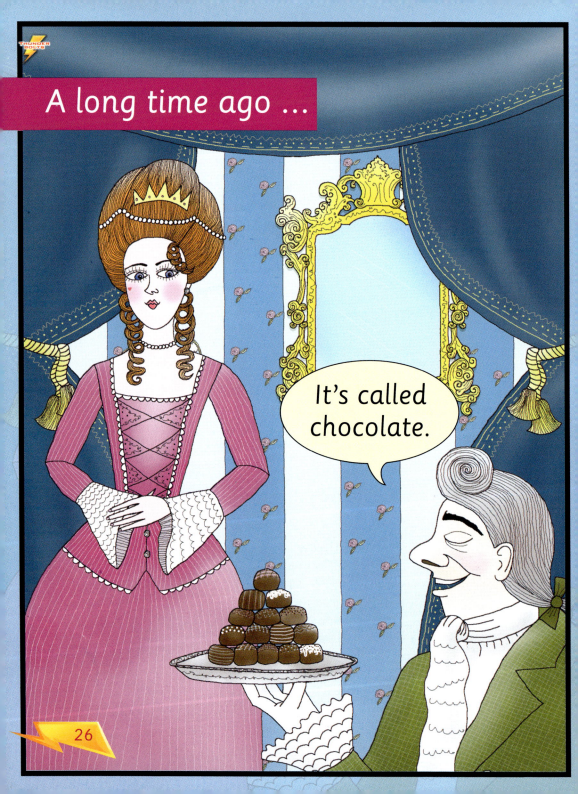

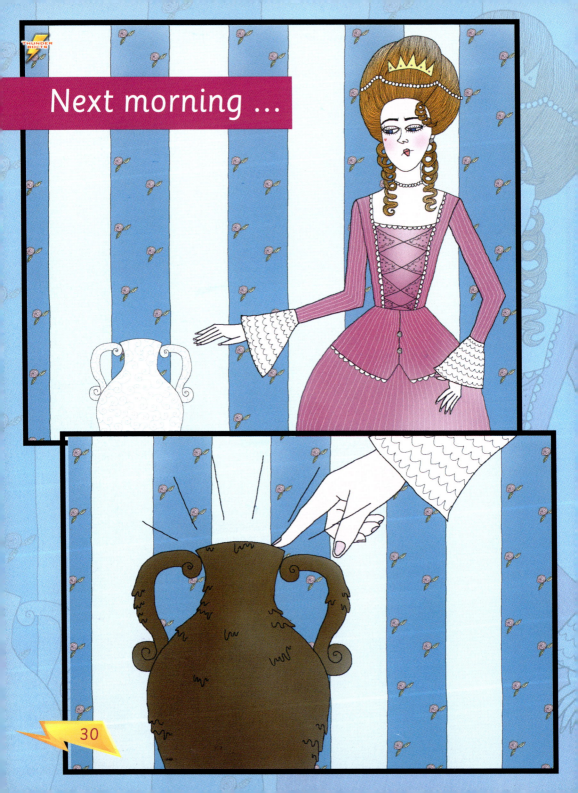

The wish had come true!

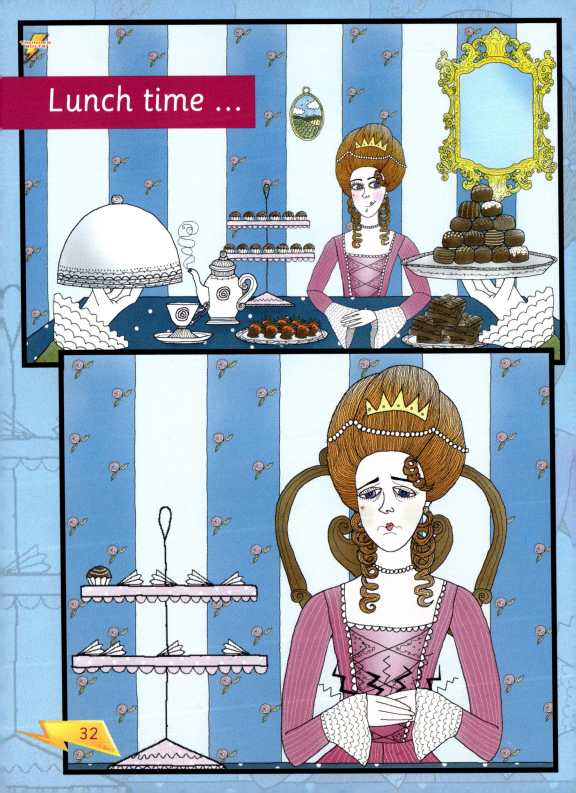

Lunch time …

That night ...

No more!

34

Word list

bee

chocolate

cocoa

cream

drinking

fair

flower

honey

lunch

nectar

powder

rationing

sugar

sweet

tasty

trade

truffle